I0568482

Through Yonder Window Breaks

Through Yonder Window Breaks

Antony Di Nardo

Wet Ink Books

First Edition

A 2021 Don Gutteridge Poetry Award Winner

Wet Ink Books
www.WetInkBooks.com
WetInkBooks@gmail.com

Through Yonder Window Breaks
by Antony Di Nardo

Cover Art – Ann Di Nardo
Cover Design – Richard M. Grove
Layout and Design – Richard M. Grove

Typeset in Garamond
Printed and bound in Canada
Distributed in USA by Ingram,
        – to set up an account – 1-800-937-0152

Library and Archives Canada Cataloguing in Publication

Title: Through yonder window breaks / Antony Di Nardo.
Names: Di Nardo, Antony, 1949- author.
Description: Poems.
Identifiers: Canadiana 20220216851 | ISBN 9781989786659 (softcover)
Classification: LCC PS8607.I535 T57 2022 | DDC C811/.6—dc23

To friends,
near and far.

Table of Contents

Window Breaks

Window Breaks

Bloomsday

Window panes shake off the rain, can take it,
Keep out the part of weather
That stains the gardens green.

It's Bloomsday on the other coast
And here I am an exile in lockdown, my odyssey
Bound by borders only minutes away.

The border a curtain for keeping out
Daylight, dim today under pensive clouds,
The sky concealed.

Each room of the house hints at finding harbour,
A bed or a chair, a corner of the universe
Where I leave my things. Every room

Sufficient to furnish a record of where I have and
Haven't been, a window in each with an inside-out
And a book I put back on the shelf.

A Poem That's More About Me Than Birds

I like to watch as much as listen—
The crackle and dance of fires at night to distance the stars.

The crows when they announce themselves in pairs
And the houselights when they go on.

The gulls that I remember ripping a seam in the sky
And squeezing through until they disappeared.

The banter and bluster of wings painting leaves.

The tear between two clouds and the sounds I heard
Telling me to wait for the geese to re-appear.

But they don't, not the ones I was expecting—
I've confused the words around my house

With the words inside my head.

Window Dressing

Either the scene pasted at the window
Obstructs the view
Or you have to look right through
To see it for yourself—

Windows all the rage
When it comes to clarity. Like jazz
They don't differentiate between light and dark,
Up or down, the phoebe or the finch.

Birds are marvellous
When cradled in the arms of a tree,
Fluid and harmless when they fly.
You can tell they have a way

With wings but not much
Of a threshold when it comes to breaking glass.
Music always sounds like music
When you listen to them sing

However, they can't come through
A window just on a whim.
Sure, glass is made to disappear,
But only if you know where and how to look.

Snowscape

with a line by Charles Wright

A snowscape at my window this morning,
bright and early, laid out like a blanket
well   before the birds have found their voices.

It may be coincidental, but I'm thinking about
my friend, Robert Walzer, from long ago,
whom I usually called Bob except on occasions
when I introduced him at readings,
his specialty, imagery in theatre of the absurd.

His family came from Wengen, a place high up
in the Swiss Alps from where we'd take the cable car
to Lauterbrunnen for a day of hiking.

We had bread and cheese with us, apples
and a cucumber, drank from streams along the way
or chewed on mittfuls of melting snow.

He talked about our lunch in detail as if it were poetry
on a Sunday picnic—how we quenched our thirst
on snowmelt and how satisfying a cucumber can be,
four or five bites in the right order, always a thing
of beauty, and how caffeine in the DNA of an apple
provided a powerful boost to metaphoric activity.

Description, he would say (air quotes materializing
between the peaks), the least appreciated of all the arts.

I think Bob, his appetite profound, his mind never weary,
would enjoy what I'm seeing outside my window today—
a snowscape, bright and early, waiting to be devoured.

Five Selected Scenes of Winter at the Window

1

No bigger than a foot
The sharp-shinned hawk
Falls into my boot
And pulls out a sock

Gripped in its talons
Two shades of yellow
My sock ablaze, the sky
A shocking glow

2

It's a quiet shade of mid-morning woodland gray, the
hemlock green but dull and variable—I can taste a coming
storm in the air that's metal on the tongue—the wind
picking up its bow, now with a long *andante* across the level
branches, now a *largo* strummed like the woods had given
this some thought

3

In the beginning birds
gave us the words
for flitter
and flutter,
for the flute
and flicker of wing tip
to wing tip,
for the long graceful swoop
of a hand,
unfettered,
ungloved,
uncluttered,
turning the page

4

What if nothing moved for a day?
Nothing at all
Like sci-fi nothing
Not the boughs at the window
Nor the pots in the kitchen
Not even the baseboard heater
                given to raising the temperature
What if nothing moved, nothing at all, while I was away?

5

A black-capped member of
The family tree

My baby-blue toque on
The crown of the coat rack

A white-breasted nuthatch on
Gray-tipped wings

Hot coals in the fire box
Smoke on the rise

Tall-leggèd maples bare
Heads in the clouds

Syllable

Winter begins
like any other winter
that falls
through the trees
and fills the air
at the window,
lays itself down
in varying depths
of being
flat out
on the ground,
and says what it is
in plain, simple
language,
talks to itself
and talks to all who trudge,
slow-footed,
heavy-footed,
sinking deeper
into its deep-down element,
a syllable like no other,
said softly, quietly
through the woods
and on the high hills,
when it brings down the sky,
the sky at our feet.

Blue Spruce

The frozen pond I cut across
reflects the moon at noon
when winter followed me here.

A man who walks on eggshells
cracking jokes about himself
does not entertain the topic of a shelf life.

I hit the deck where folks are most at home.
Insulated walls.
Firs and bushy tails.

Homegrown greens and woolens.
Space heaters fashioned out of broken sticks
to beat back the cold.

And above me, a star-like fish,
the winter sun
swimming out of its depths.

Tomorrow has been predicted.
I stitch together jam and jazz for an indoor picnic.
I raise a totem to thoughts

of lingering, sing of how the blue spruce got its name.
I linger. Winter stuffed inside a glove
like a pair of birds I can't explain.

Sleeper

I sit in second class, at my desk,
window side
with a panorama of snow mounds,
snow boughs,
the backyard
back and forth of winter birds
filling up at their stations.

A dull day if I've ever seen one,
gray sky,
an empty coffee mug,
gray wings
over the deep dank gloom
of a sorry memory
I obliterate when I draw
the curtains shut.

A Short Story

Already the day has quit and I'm wishing for more.
The only means I have of understanding why
I'm here are disconnected and I can't forget
they culminate without a trace of what comes next.

I see myself in charge of snow, the image is of great
expanse, of winter wares compressed in vague ideas
of widespread solitude. It really is quite dark, the night
accomplished and unseen, shedding levels of diffusion.

But so what? I'm tongue-tied in the here and now,
with the gloaming attributes of darkness that surface
at the window as the lights go out. There's meaning to be
found in the pointlessness of a quiet night alone at home

but not before the moon, a fine moon, Hemingways
into the room and throws itself across the bed.

Approximately 6:30 pm

Some Saturday
in December
facing north
and losing light

early dusk,
the air
like anywhere else
here on Earth

news of the world
guaranteed to reach
my network feed,
I draw the blinds,
conclusions,
the windows
leaking
thickened
shadows

the gloom
meant for me
to understand
the meaning of
dark,
darker and
darkness

Wipe Out

We wipe out the carnivores so we can have all the meat to ourselves.

Wipe out the clouds for an afternoon to flatter our bodies.

Wipe out the bees.

Wipe out disease (heart burns and fungus and sickle cell anemia)
                                    just to live up to the cusp of forever.

Wipe out the negative from the positive and our debt to the future.

Wipe out the coral and chords of the sea that our muses sing.

We wipe it all out so we'll know how it ends and we won't be surprised,
                                                    or disappointed.

Network

I can't google
what I'm feeling,
how to surface
and devour
the me
from inside out,
to disconnect
my endocrinal network
of impediments
to see exposed
on the windows
of a 13-inch
touch screen.

No way, not now,
in any case
AI can't quite get
just yet
to the bottom
of the wellspring
and pull up
all the self-help stuff
that we apply to states
of mind, the cauliflower
convolutions of gray
and twisted matter,
dendrites sinking deeper
in darker places
released to signal when
I've gone off
the grid.

And outside the window
above my head
between the clouds,
silver wings
completely disconnected
yet airborne.

After a Painting by Marc Chagall and a Piece by Miles Davis

the night lingers
and "So What"
fills the room

the spilled wine
empty bottle
the broken glass

so many pages more
to fill, for me
to conjure

into reason
summoning myself
back to NYC

and nights
of moon-soaked lovers
flying

out of bedroom windows

The Mountain That Appears in My Poem
for Miguel

The mountain that appears in my poem
is the mountain that appears in every poem I write.
I take it with me wherever I go.

To be neither here nor there is a powerful thing
                              if you stay in one place.

Some say "place" as if it's all they know—
what they call home, a place in their heart,
                              their place in a queue.

I am free to write because I am not a threat
to anyone or anything—my words are never meant
                    to hurt or change places with you.

When I reached the summit of the mountain that
appears in my poem I saw the opposite side
of the valley but no one was there to greet me—
they were all at home hiding their faces.

It's a mystery to me
            why people in my poem hide their faces.

I think it's safe to say the mountain will still be there
                              when I'm done writing.

Does the mountain know it has a place in my poem?

I think it's safe to say it doesn't understand the question.

Condo Listing

One flag waltzing, the other
tilted into a minimal breeze. Spring,
as if to say, winter's gone at last.

A billboard hides her face
and a rooftop A-C unit. Two fingers
of rain fall in a porcelain cup.

Balcony planters lay about wasted,
waiting, wanting sunlight – the dirt
cracked and caked in clumps.

Eager, the birds make illiterate zigzags
of the air, her tenant's eyes following
feathers here and footsteps there.

God knows what racket in a distant
bell, Anglican, or the clang of beer
cans in the parking lot below. Cars

cramped in rows, irritants by the blight
of slamming doors, a building with years
of broken specs between the floors.

The buzz of insects, door bells,
the snapping open-shut of beaks, gulls
neck to neck on a nearby lamppost. Caw-caw.

Nothing else to see but people rushed
and bagged by the weight of shopping
carts and dinner-minded purpose. She

leans to look down from the balcony perched
at First and Albert just above the brink
of a bank soon to vacate 700 sq. ft.

of condo space with the misplaced smell
of beaver puke compressed in Billy
bookshelves by Ikea. An eviction notice

sticky-tacked to the door. Third floor.
Ensuite. Sliding windows. Electric fireplace.
Marble counters. Storage.

Decisions

Come at a cost.

They weigh you down.
They turn your head.
They catch you napping.

That crease in your forehead.
That thing you do with the volume.
Ageing along with the wine that's in no way as old as you.

Your eyes concealed within the pages of a book.
The trail of crumbs you leave behind.
We've all been there, on the horns of a dilemma

Or in the middle a conversation
And we're not even talking about the same thing.
I confess.

I went hunting when I was 23 or 24
And shot a partridge.
I ate the poor thing.

Approximating Dawn

When the little light comes on
it's obvious I know what it means to be human—
where to put my head,
my slippers, the pot of coffee,
what to say about the birds hitting all the right notes.

Glass at the window as an element of the stars
accordions the light. The curtains remember
an open window.
Strings of violets mention the morning breeze
beyond the walls.

And above the roofline, rising, the lusty boughs of
a hemlock hard at work,
sacred to the rosy glow of morning
air-brushed to illuminate the ends of the earth.

I know for a fact how many raisins in a kilo.
How many moments in a minute.
What's out there when the sunlight's on.
I know the instrument I have inside my head
can playback the day before and before the day is done
I will have gone away with it and then come back.

How human of me to have noticed where the morning
shows its face on the mountainside.

Call it dawn, sunrise, daybreak —it happens
every time I take the milk out of the fridge
                            and the little light comes on.

Window Breaks

Beirut Port Explosion, 4 August 2020

three thousand years to make this glass
a thousand more to stain it
a lifetime looking out
through yonder window panes
where glass is engineered
                                        to disappear

glass that dislocates and then connects
relaxes, flows
uninterrupted in a city
at my desk, across the years and sunk
into these limpid eyes

                        until broken

broken into a million shards
a million tongues
                        a million dreams lost
            in smithereens of kaleidoscopic
cuts and slits
            bits and barbs unbound
                        in beads and beads of
beaten combinations, busted fierce
as fragments on the icy water's face
            slivers in a bombed-out heart
the grimace of a shattered city
                                    raining shrapnel
on a hot and sunny summer's day

Room with a View

These things don't mean a thing—
beauty, Bolshevism, broken hearts—
if you're dead.

But if you're not then
you're a speck of wildlife, a moment's wick
connected to your time on earth as meaningful

as giving birth to picturing the moon
a crescent when you look outside your window
and there's nothing else to think about.

Rejection

Nature tells us everything once
Geoffrey Nutter

What do these trees mean
when they lose their leaves,
tearful through the cycling
of the seasons?

      Absolutely nothing.

Their long sighs never leave
them out of breath. There are
no rules for how to bend
their trunks, nod their heads,
kiss the air goodbye. And they're
okay with that. They calculate
sums in rings, grow fond of light,
nests and home deliveries.
There's a bit of them in me.

Once when I was twelve and
confused, tangled in the twisted
turns and sinews of its arms,
I hung from a tree like these,
a rope wrapped around my neck,
and it had the nerve to spit me out.

But I, a child of twelve, persisted,
kept returning, climbed its branches
insistent that I should be its fruit to bear.
I was a child then, a mere twig of a boy
who survived, now I write not to forget
the tree that would not have him.

The Snail

In a forest of tall slender maples,
dips and craters the size of a moon,
I felt no bigger than a pebble.

The sap was cooling and moving
slowly like a curl of smoke.
No faster.

I ran a red light in a world
completely devoid of red lights.
No one knew.

I had reason to believe in the impossible.
My chassis as I found out was branded
with a Fibonacci sequence.

As if it needed an explanation.
As if a little engine ran my heart
and horizons were impossible to reach.

Homophones Are Real

The universe doesn't have
any use for doors,
so I look out my window instead
and count the stars from here

Call me ridiculous,
but I like the trembling sensation
of finding something
for the very first time—

the light, for example

a poem by Pessoa (but written by someone else)

or flower and flour in the very same sentence

A Walking Sonnet

with a line by Jules Renard

My coffee's rich in colour and warm
and I'm thinking how nature's got my back
just as I belong on nature's back, I,
hospitable and kind, open the door

and go out walking, the body moving
forward while the mind flutters around it
like a bird that lands on this and that,
on evergreens of fresh ideas and snippets

stretched from branch to branch, words
eventually inserted back into the kitchen
and cranked into a pattern at the window,
gibberish at first but soon enough a thrill

to follow where the birds have taken me,
knowing I've never had this thought before.

The Mountain Refuge

All mountains gather in a single peak,
all the roads together
lead us there and back into our kitchens
where desires long for comfort
in the face of hunger, thirst,
a peeled banana
given up as sacrifice to mend our empty stomachs.

Boots matched up in pairs and stationed at the door.

Anoraks hung on hooks for when the weather
                              looks the other way.

A list of names of those who've come and gone.

A place to sit before we leave.

Elvis the Mountain

The rain pours out of heaven
in long strands of silvers and grays—

the work of the mountain, combing it back
and heaping it up in the valleys.

(The sky for the purpose of this poem
is made up mostly of feathers and curls.)

A clock sticks out its tongue,
licking its lips, gathering clouds.

The trees are naked, straight and tall,
the road is an uphill climb.

The leaves will return with an urge
to get out and leave the house.

Evening is about to cross my mind
trapped in the delicate balance

between twilight and dusk.
If I move my head this way or that

the window falls out of sight
and the mountain has left the building.

Red

for Tai

That colour,
that one and only
colour, occupies
centre stage
and takes a bow.

That one colour,
burning hot as fire
up against the curtain
drawn tight
and white as snow.

That one fire, stark
and bright as the flag
on a white-tailed deer,
bounding up and gone
beneath the boughs.

That leap, sharp
as eyes can read
the contrast,
two colours juxtaposed
and real as winter—

the true north strong
and heading for the trees.

Zooming

At this distance you cannot feel
the beauty of my heart.

My aura you must agree is indistinct
even if we have the same books on the shelf
and share the same time zones.

In the space between body and spirit
we get closer to being look-alike Venn diagrams.

We are here on earth to intersect and overlap.

Yes, my darling, like rain and water,
birds and bird beaks.

Over One's Head

There is enough weather in these parts to satisfy the majority,
every nuance of falling snow,
every tortured wind-blown speck of sand is reported,
every blush of petal,
the look in the eye of the sun on a Sunday.

There are so many versions but none as true
as the one you believe in.

Some of us are wild enough for two.

But weather is often biblical and reported on the actual date
as the story of a life that live streams past your window.

It is put into words as one,
as one thing only, comprehensive and all-encompassing,
like *ceiling*
written without an inkling of what there is to see when you look up.

Clean White Shirt

Unlike a gust of wind that's clocked in passing
by and passing time that won't sit still,
I'm held on "Hold" and put on "Pause"
when faced with moving on.

The day unfolds, I'm a clean white shirt,
the night a trembling mess of sleeves,
dark and troubled until I shut my eyes
and vanish on a hook behind the door.

Then morning comes and someone takes
my place where the kitchen table soaks
the light and I can't tell from where I hang
what's changed or still the same.

Life List

Another person might not leave
their desk for weeks
the sun setting over the same few trees,
the same trees that have been here
with the very same names
for as long as we've been counting rings,
a conclusion to the idea
of where it all ends, and
the moon constant and happy as a pearl
hanging over Pierre's newly painted shingles
where the same pair of Eastern phoebes
nesting at his window
have been there since day one last year.

I'm sorry to disappoint but I have nothing new
to add to my list of sightings
although I can imagine birds
like the Korean magpie
and European coal tit
in the branches of a tree
that another poet*
snagged closer
to a portion of the sky
I could never reach,
the distance to my front door
farther than I expected.

*Robert Hass in "Seoul Notebook"

Breathing

Chirring as a hawk
might chirr, spiral
as its wings collapse,
beak in prey mode.

Stirring, waking mid
of night, asking am I where
I think I am
in this abundance of darkness.

I probe, you probe,
we all probe
for a pulse, the hunter
and the hunted alike.

When cones of sleep return
I fill in blanks and
cover up the holes
my life exposed

And I come back
to breathing
as the one thing
I am really good at.

Purdy's Place

The poet repeats the patience of water
in a line from a text

he's left on the desk—that fish need know
nothing of currents to swim.

He matches words to the measure of the moon
their eyes contain.

The weather over Lake Ontario
rests in his hands.

Ridges on his cheeks trace patterns
consistent with the lines he writes.

He sounds the soup of rain thinning as it falls
and then swallows it whole.

Birds bend behind his head
and swim the air each within its laws.

The thick of meadows, the woodland draws,
he takes them off when he goes to bed.

Exorbitant the stars at night—
those that linger at his window.

A Higher Power

If there's a higher power
I'm looking at her—green
on a hot summer's day

of rain, on and in between
her leaves stroked by sunlight
when the switch is on. The joe

pie weed and asters line
the land bridge and repeat
themselves in how I picture

them in words for mother, sister,
brother, the angle of the earth
at latitude 51.2 degrees, and trees

that rub their cheeks against the sky
where birds leave their nests behind
and the hydro lines can't reach.

Fall,
an Orange
and a Piece of String

Fall

The Government fell to a clash of colours,

the leaves unified at last when they gathered
on the square, grounded
to a mulch of grave decompositions, dull and beige.

By comparison, the rains were green and lingered
for nine months before they turned to snow,
a hint of dusk on a wintry brow.

A lovely violet colour came between the setting sun
and stars that night, the leaves, one moment quick
with chlorophyll, gone when the wind puffed out its cheeks.

The Leaves Are Falling

It's fall again
closing in on second thoughts
and rusty philosophies—
evidence as empirical
and Descartes as unavoidable.

Fall again.
Disturbances at the borders
ten kliks from Vermont,
no kliks from the rain—
being born has now been done
and the rest
is up to me.

Fall again.
Bach and Bobby Curtola,
the poetry Bobs,
what more can they say?—

The leaves are falling,
the leaves are falling
and ours to keep.

The Evergreens of Autumn

You render leaves in colour on your cell,
I use my pen.

Who else sees what you do?
Who else knows where I look?

Leaves come down raining big fat flakes
before either of us ever gets to say another word.

There's a spell we know that changes water into shades of red,
gold and amber, green ferns turned to brass.

And everywhere the evergreens,
their deep, dark green that's everlasting,

know too well
Autumn is that time for keeping to themselves.

Duck Pond

It doesn't take long for the pond
to swim out to sea even with the sea
a thousand miles from where it starts.

The journey crosses mountains, meadows,
the minds of people on the street,
settlers, followers, mighty chasms,

the greedy and abandoned drowning
where the waters flow,
hopes and deliberations,

the town of Duncan, the border,
even the city of Boston,
before it exits and tastes the salt of the sea

in the mix of brine and life that swims,
the ooze of mud and bone, the waves
a miracle of assimilation, blood, peace,

equality, the dead and living alike,
the living sucking on the same
sea-stirred air as the ducks on the pond.

Tail Wagging

I tackle happiness with utmost care—
I once allowed *Notre-Dame* to break my heart,
Afghanistan to wring me dry, country music
to make it all better.

I take the lead whenever I can, the happiest of days
those that come from the bottom up, days that look
to the sky with the least little fuss.
Wings take me there, wings take me back.

And on the esplanade outside my window a beautiful
white-haired man calls his dog, pulls on the lead, the dog
impersonating the happiness of one who wags his tail,
while the gulls guffaw at the sight of being tethered.

Groom

When was the last time I took myself
down the aisle? Looking for a shortcut,
passed the checkout, out the exit before

I stop for the sake of stopping to consider
the ripeness of melons, the specials
on sensations. What else is on my mind?

How can a shopping list exist at all?
How long have I been doing this? I ask
the shopper standing inside the glass

next to where I wait. I've met myself
in the future and I know that my co-ordinates
are here. I know what husband has come to mean.

The one to push the cart, who leaves just when
I do. I'm collecting points with every purchase
that I make and what's more human than that?

Home on the Range

Arrows and frigates
Nuclear missiles, F-18s
IEDs and submarines
Bullets and muskets
Daggers and drones
Rifles and pot-shots
Any killing machine—
These are the least
Of my favorite things
When the sky
Is all cloudy and grey

Approximately 8 p.m.

It's the hour before the sun begins to set
and the sky has no idea what to do with itself,
white as a sheet that's seen a ghost.

I wrote my future on the last remaining clouds
but like all of us they were on their way out.

Besides, who'd be left to read my words in the dark
unless darkness was the word you were looking for.

Coffee and Bird

Coffee and bird this morning, both about the same
—back and forth in my corpus callosum

I sip on sparrows
    said the early spring

I taste their songs
    said the rainclouds licking leaves

I feel their wings
    said the trembling boughs

I smell coffee
    said the rose nodding at the window

It's flown away
    said my empty cup

Burgeoning

The sun, the morning mine,
an unmade bed

Frugal of both what's said
and left unsaid

Ragged leaves

Dog's breath

Cedarwood and ragweed

Standing on both feet,
a notion I'm a tree about to burst

a split second
away from getting started

My Leaf

My face, my hair, my arms
freckled with tens of thousand times
more days behind me now
than when I was much younger

My colour, my shape and vessel

The trestle of my bearing

Hive and honey, belly full

Eyes ablaze, the mind
a wonder-plus of autumn leaf

Borne by both my "then" and "now"

Twisting in the air before it lands

Eclogue for a Sunday Afternoon

I don't doubt birds
sing in key
and the *hemerocallis fulva*
is a perfect blend of red
and yellow blossoms,
whatever other colour
we imagine them to be,
with the average cost
of garden maintenance
a weary back
and dab of antiphlogistine rub,
the grasses tamed
and whipper-snapped
back into shape
with the *grrr* and fuel-injected
growl of lawn appliances
put to test my patience
one last time
so clouds can softly, gently
pass me by.

Passion

"Earth, O fecund, thou" says an old poem*
and I tell the trees all about it

I've instructed them to appear in the language of colour
The glint in the eyes of leaves in the fall

I remind them all creatures are crazy with desire
The leaves after a summer of passion

At the end they let go, fall with an urge to touch and taste
the ground, transcend the tree and their attachments

*a poem by Frank Bidart

Dissidence

You won't find dissidents in the natural world.
Don't bother looking. No thing or being objects
to you or one another. Don't let the crow fool you.
That's not its purpose. Or the yellowing leaves

on a maple. The sky is not falling and
the measure of clouds is erasure. Soon, winter
will scab a skin on the puddles and break us
down into binaries of hot and cold, in and out.

But that's not dissidence, that's home, a boreal
glade, a window and its opposites.

Keeping Quiet

It felt like December—
or as close as we could get to it—
the darkest month,
the one we drive into with our lights on fire.

There's opposition and then there's confrontation.
I know the difference—this evening, cold and weary,
I asked a motorist parked outside my door
to turn her engine off.

She called me an idiot, and added a few more expletives.
I thought about that for a while, her choice
of words—wondering how I can improve upon
what can't be left unsaid.

Another Odyssey

My brother's dead
as of ten o'clock last night—
he had nowhere else to go.

Over the balcony, a thousand
motivations, back and forth
across the street,

some parked in SUVs
for the greatest journey on earth
that goes from Aaa! to Zzz!

there is no one alive anymore
who remembers me as a baby
is a line I love

in a poem by Louise Glück
that feeds the fragments
of my memory

of when my brother lived
and parked his car
across the street.

House Clearing

They're all dead.
I've wracked my brains to find them.
They're all dead.
Aunts and uncles.
Neighbours on the street.
The purple starlings on the line.
They're all dead.
Dead as our kitchen table
And seven chairs
Raised upon an island
Not so easily forgotten.
Yet none of them can remember
The river that meandered
And the names of those
Who took the chairs away.

The Fall

Who can shake the thought
of another headline,
the last century,
teddy bears
and flowers at the gates
just to say
everything's okay, my dear,
go back to bed,
don't mention
that you've got a gun
and where you keep your bullets safe,
one without the other
makes for another
peaceful day
in the country,
the susurration
of mid-October leaves
about to leap into the air,
fall and hit the ground
just as you'd expect to happen
when someone shoots you dead.

The Red Planet

I land in a painted forest enchanted with scarlet leaves
and golden boughs

The locals have given names to every tree

The yellow birches talk in tongues, catch on fire

The beeches sag without compromise

The ash and hemlock touch in shades of green

And maples, that resist the pull of gravity
for as long as they can, go red in the face for trying

When the leaves let go I stuff my pockets, fill my head

I radio back to ground control

Poems That Appear in Almanacs

Poems that appear in almanacs are there
to predict the future

They send you hiking up 3000 feet one day,
collect your thoughts the next

Tell you when to expect the apples in the apple tree
to finally grow up

They list the years when history loved a revolution

Compare the two, the junior and the senior,
with Bush the second coming out as quite the peach

You'll find portraits of a bathtub,
lyrics on the beach,
haikus on the up and coming phases of the moon,
epics on breaking bread,
tankas on reading tea leaves,
titles such as *Sic Parvis Magna*,
odes to candle sticks without a wick,
premonitions of the harvest

And places where a poem hides
when you come looking for another

Weightlessly

Too bad Emily Dickinson
Doesn't know where I live—
Doesn't know what I want

Too bad—
I'd love to hear
What she'd have to say

If only she were here with me
Beneath the trees—
Writing *Weightlessly*

And reading it out loud—
So that even the leaves
Might know what it is I want

Of Potato Peels and Poetry

1

Potato peels, my chimney sweep tells me,
contain sufficient potassium
to wipe away at least 5%
of built-up creosote in my flu.

How many potato peels need I burn, I ask.
Oh, about 50-60 pounds, he says,
                give or take.

2

Erasure, the deliberate
removal of writing
where you end up with 50-60% less
(maybe more) of the original
                with only 5% effort.

3

"Learn about bamboo from the bamboo"
Basho said, and the poem will follow.

4

Poetry is slow and gradual,
sometimes in the likeness of a bamboo grove,
sometimes grown out of something else,
much like soot soon turns to creosote,
much like finding the right words in the right order—
which is what
        Samuel Taylor Coleridge wrote.

Synonym

It's been hours since a stranger's gone by,
Begins a poem
That begins when a stranger goes by.

The writer reaches for a sense of wonder,
Clears a place inside a poem, evidence
A sky is shared by looking up when one goes by.

If colours in a box of colours begin a painting,
Then either way, true or false,
A stranger looking at the sky sees one too
When a cloud goes by.

A day in progress—there are never two the same—
Writes itself into the poem,
Takes the word for stranger as synonym
For when a cloud goes by.

Clarity, Ontario

I held on.

I had fallen back
an hour the day before
and this morning
Lake Ontario hid behind
a metallic tint
not shimmering
but flat like a dull
and filthy blade
the wind had yet
to scour clean.

Mighty plumes
towered
over the eastern pier
pummeled
by the mightier force
of pounding waves
stabbing into the mettle
of a like-minded universe
equivalent to hurricane
and tempest framed
in the easy comfort
of a metaphor.

(extra-
ordinary never felt
so paralyzing)

The waves came at me
full force
full fathom
crashing dizzy
high against the pier
where lights dazzled
and clouds collapsed
                    the air
wet with spray and
piercing drizzle
the docks consumed
by wind and wake
white caps and curl
stunned by chaos
knocking down
the coast of clarity.

And when I turned
to walk away
the wind with its arm
around my waist
held me back—

I had no other
place to be.

On a Clear Night in September, Looking Up at the Sky with the Moon Off to One Side

What's the one word we all know?
Is it *Time*? Or its opposite?
How much farther or how much longer?

There's the night before and the day right after.
The gloaming and the restlessness of impermanence
if we wait too long to find the right word.

Only who, I ask you, can wait this long
(a lifetime by my calculations)
before another star, another sun

brightens the moon, that embryo
for the songs we sing
when light through yonder window breaks?

A Visit from Time to Time

Mind-altering, soul-shifting, life-changing events
happen in the past.

I look out of autumn windows and see trees differently
from one day to the next.

I look down the block and one day no one's there
the next they've all come back.

I feel like I've been pushed into a book by Stephen King.

What's happening, that things don't stay the same?

Another leaf.
Another songbird with a chorus in reverse.
Another jet plane.

The coffee grounds in the kitchen sink.

It's all moving, moving, moving
like time itself is going down the drain.

The Histories

The moon, full shine, fell out of sight
before I could bring it to your attention.

You were sleeping, the sun barely up,
resting its head on your pillow.

Rosy red, I said, a lunar eclipse
the likes of which had never been seen

since the birth of Henry VI
re-appearing a few centuries later

while you slept in our bed,
the glow from the light on your face

oblivious to cosmic phenomena
or the histories of England.

Yesterday

I'm not one to look beyond rooflines—
nothing there but the emptiness of empty space.

At the end of the day
the lights at Third and Albert remain the same,
remind me that the irony of a blurry vision
was once a sweeping glance.

It seems I might be right.
There are no stars tonight above the rooftops.
No November moon to think about.

People passing by will eventually collapse
into the past, and if not now in the years to come.

Can you imagine Paul McCartney singing that?

Perhaps the Stars Are Paperclips

Perhaps they are just what I need
to keep two thoughts together

Perhaps they bend the light
to keep the darkness in its place

Perhaps they serve no purpose whatsoever
like stardust and wishful thinking

Perhaps there's more to stars
than twinkling, shimmering and outer space

Perhaps that's how it is with ordinary things
like paperclips and starry nights

Mathematics for Small Sums

A broken pot
Earth
Spilling out its
Molecules
That add up to something
With a label
And then that's it
That's all there is
To filling in
The empty
Space

Fixed

I'm one of two
Or three
Or seven billion people who know
Where to look for possibilities
Objects of love
Decisions
Mathematical delights
The voice of a songbird
The weight of a bee
The height of a tree
At exactly 45.10 degrees
North and 72.61 degrees
West

Darkness, Approximated

A blur of leaves, like ships across the pond.
A memory passing, like nothing ever happened.
Remembering—just to know I can.

The trees upright, decisively
So green and bursting with the expertise of CO2
Gathering lakes of shade until the sun's connection's lost.

Then darkness like I could never imitate
Or feel that I could be as clearly understood as that.
Or find another word to mean the same.

Apostrophe

I work hard at writing, like a carpenter drilling a hole
with a safety pin and mitering a joint
that puts two pieces of a desk together.

When the desk is done I open the drawer
and stuff my poems in.

I work hard at making English my first language.
I also speak sky, rock and water, but those come easily.

I work hard at creating firescapes,
diminishing a stack of kindling piled behind the garden shed
next to words I wrote and pinned up on the wall.

I work hard at that.

I work hard at remembering names, titles, articles of birth,
that time I walked into a bar and made a joke.

I work hard at re-writing the sea of Lake Ontario, salmon
leaping, clouds colliding.

There's a convention in poetry that addresses the reader.

I work hard at doing that.

Canto

Today I swear the fall is all slang,
its mouth wet with the way
it picks out colours, speaks
in tongues dipped in sun.

And when it gives the words
for yellow and red
as scarlet and gold,
behold, the leaves appear

and the little blue
and green of the sky that remain
linger only in the sentence
I just wrote.

An Orange and a Piece of String

... I am greatly astonished at God's imagination: an imagination attuned to infinitesimal and discordant variations, as though the great question was to bring together, one day, an orange and a piece of string, a wall and a glance.

Louis Aragon, Paris Peasant

Here I sit in solitude,
one of many today
who sits in solitude,
I am certain of it,
astride the pillows
of a couch with walls
and windows
all around me,
examining
in just a glance
the amber, scarlet,
rose and gold
of autumn leaves
seen at a latitude
north of someone
south of me and east
of where you are.
I name the colours
one by one and one by one
they begin to fall.

It's all the same to me,
this talk of leaves, the sun,
the roots and fruit
that bind the trees
to common ground,
one word after another
falling from the sky,
and I sit back and follow
them until I reach
the bottom of the page.

I am no prescient God,
yet I know precisely how
these words come to an end
and how they got their start—
with an orange
and a piece of string.

Notes and Acknowledgments

The line by Charles Wright in *Snowscape* is "description, the least appreciated of all the arts."

The line I borrowed from Jules Renard in the poem, *A Walking Sonnet*, is "walking, the body moving forward while the mind flutters around it like a bird."

I am grateful to the editors of the following journals and anthologies where some of these poems first appeared: Devour, Event, Envoy, Poetry Present, and Spirit of the Hills Anthology.

My thanks to Don Gutteridge for having selected this work for publication in the 2021 inaugural Don Gutteridge Poetry Award, and to John B. Lee, Jessica Outram and James Pickersgill for their initial review of the manuscript. And, as always, a big hug to Richard (Tai) Grove for being the maestro that enables and conducts these many compositions into books.

This book would not exist without Annie, whose art and sensibility not only appears on the cover but informs every new day with her very own light and love.

Author Statement

Three poets converged on my psyche when I was but a pup and left an indelible impression: John Donne, because of his sweeping metaphysics and mastery of form; e.e. cummings, because of his playfulness with language and experimentation; and Leonard Cohen, because of his emotional chutzpah and utter lack of sentimentality. As I grew into the art and craft of poetry, influential poets doubled in numbers, then tripled, and now are too numerous to list, although in my greying years giants like James Tate, Mary Ruefle, and Al Purdy continue to inform my work in different ways.

I've always been attracted to nature, as much as to the surreal and the absurd, and I believe that like any work of art, "a poem should not mean but be." So much of what I write tends in that direction, creating a work that is defined by its own internal systems, that is inward looking as much as it relies on its external referents to be appreciated. Language has a built-in wow factor: words are not only signifiers for the seemingly-endless manifestations of the world, but they also come with integrated audio. Words make sounds, and, when I write, those sounds figure as much as the images in my broken lines.

Through Yonder Window Breaks, like my other books, bears testimony to both classical and contemporary influences. Some of these poems shatter glass into a million pieces, others, I believe, do such a fine job of cleaning windows that you can see right through them.

Publication List:

Alien, Correspondent (Brick Books, 2010)
Soul on Standby (Exile Editions, 2010)
Roaming Charges (Brick Books, 2015)
SKYLIGHT (Ronsdale Press, 2018)
Gone Missng (Hidden Brook Press, 2020)
Forget-Sadness-Grass (Ronsdale Press, 2022)

Author Bio

Antony Di Nardo is the author of six books of poetry, most recently, Forget-Sadness-Grass (Ronsdale Press, 2022). In addition to being a finalist for the CBC Poetry Prize, his work has won the Gwendolyn MacEwen Poetry Award for best suite of poems and was nominated for a National Magazine Award. Many of his poems appear in journals and anthologies across Canada and internationally, and have been translated into several languages. A former teacher of English and creative writing, he was born in Montreal and lives in Cobourg, Ontario.